Y0-EGE-634

Playing with Plays™
Presents
Shakespeare's

Much Ado About Nothing
FOR KIDS

(The melodramatic version!)

For 8-20+ actors, or kids of all ages who want to have fun!
Creatively modified by Brendan P. Kelso
Cover illustrated by Shana Lopez
Food Critic: Debra Williamson
Special Contributor: Ren Kris
Special Contributor: Asif Zamir

3 Melodramatic Modifications of Shakespeare's Play
for 3 different group sizes:

8-11+

12-16+

16-20+

Table Of Contents

"O this learning, what a thing it is!"
-- Taming of the Shrew, Act 1 Scene 2

via the authors of:
PursuedByABear.net
Ren Kris, Meryl Federman, and Jessi Nowack

THANK YOU!

Playing with Plays™ – Shakespeare's Much Ado About Nothing – for Kids

Copyright © 2004-2011 by Brendan P. Kelso, Playing with Publishing

Printed in the United States of America

Published by: Playing with Publishing

ISBN: 1-4538-8087-9
ISBN: 978-1453880876

Foreword

When I was in high school there was something about Shakespeare that appealed to me. Not that I understood it mind you, but there were clear scenes and images that always stood out in my mind. Romeo & Juliet, "Romeo, Romeo; wherefore art thou Romeo?"; Julius Caesar, "Et tu Brute"; Macbeth, "Double, Double, toil and trouble"; Hamlet, "to be or not to be"; A Midsummer Night's Dream, all I remember about this was a wickedly cool fairy and something about a guy turning into a donkey that I thought was pretty funny. It was not until I started analyzing Shakespeare's plays as an actor that I realized one very important thing, I still didn't understand them. Seriously though, it's tough enough for adults, let alone kids. Then it hit me, why don't I make a version that kids could perform, but make it easy for them to understand with a splash of Shakespeare lingo mixed in? And viola! A melodramatic masterpiece was created!

The entire purpose of this book is to instill the love of acting and Shakespeare into kids. I initially wrote my first Shakespeare play (Hamlet) to teach a few kids how to have fun with Shakespeare. It has evolved into a revolving door of new and returning kids constantly wanting more and more Shakespeare, from kids asking for the entire Shakespeare anthology for Christmas to writing a report in their 2nd grade class on heroes and choosing Shakespeare. Shakespeare is difficult enough when you are an adult, let alone a teenager (I didn't have a clue what Julius Caeser was about, except for "Et tu Brute!"). But for kids, most people (those calling themselves "adults" mind you) told me to forget it, "you can't teach kids Shakespeare". Well, I will have you know, that not only do these kids love Shakespeare now, they want more of it! And when you have children who have a passion for something, they will start to teach themselves, with or without school.

THE PLAYS: There are 3 plays within this book, for three different group sizes. The reason: to allow educators or parents to get the story across to their children regardless of the size of their group. Experienced actor variation: If you read any Shakespeare play as an actor you will notice one very common occurrence – NO STAGE DIRECTIONS. Okay, it happens occasionally, but it's very rare. Any actor with creative skills will tell you that this is a wonderful thing: it leaves full interpretation to the actor. Therefore, for the children who wish to explore their creative side, I suggest taking the play and whiting out ALL of the stage directions, allowing for the more experienced actors to be as creative as they want to be.

These plays are intended for pure fun. Please DO NOT have the kids learn these lines verbatim, that would be a complete waste of creativity. But do have them basically know their lines and improvise wherever they want as long as it pertains to telling the story, because that is the goal of an actor: to tell the story. In A Midsummer Night's Dream, I once had a student playing Quince question me about one of her lines, "but in the actual story, didn't the Mechanicals state that 'they would hang us'?" I thought for a second and realized that she had read the story with her mom, and she was right. So I let her add the line she wanted and it added that much more fun, it made the play theirs. I have had kids throw water on the audience, run around the audience, sit in the audience, lose their pumpkin pants (size 30 around a size 15 doesn't work very well, but makes for some great humor!) and most importantly, die all over the stage. The kids love it.

I have a basic formula that I use for these plays:
Day 1: I perform my own solo 5-minute Shakespeare play (I am totally winded by the end of it, because I have been all over the set and have died a few times if I can fit it in); we all read through the play to-gether (randomly handing out parts); then auditions – and all auditions MUST include the actors best dieing scenes (they love this the most and will line up again and again to die on stage); the other is for the screams, they love this too, but don't forget to bring earplugs, they will be incredibly loud for both girls and boys since not all have come of age yet.
Day 2: Parts are given out; we read through the play again with our new parts; start blocking
Day 3: finish blocking; rehearse
Day 4: rehearse-no scripts
Day 5: rehearse; try on costumes, and dress rehearsal
Day 6: 2 Dress rehearsals and then performance. This can easily be stretched to an 8 day course with the 2 extra days used for more rehearsal; set design; invitation creation; makeup practice; etc. As any director will tell you, actors can always use more rehearsal.

THE BARD'S WORK: As you read through the plays, there are several lines that are highlighted. These are actual lines from Shakespeare's text. I am a little more particular about the kids saying these lines verbatim. We need to do these correctly because we don't want to upset Willie. I find that there are many benefits to having these lines in there:

1. Kids are so cute when they are spouting Shakespeare.
2. Parents love to know that their kids are learning actual Shakespeare verbiage.
3. Most lines are very famous lines that they will come across later in life (to be or not to be; Romeo, Romeo, wherefore art thou; double, double toil and trouble; etc.)
4. The kids tend to feel they are more important when they are saying Shakespeare's lines.
5. The lines are easy to understand, giving the kids confidence that they will understand more Shakespeare lines later in life.

One last note: if you loved our plays, want to tell the world how much your kids loved performing Shakespeare, or are just a fan of Shakespeare, then hop on our website and have fun:

PlayingWithPlays.com

Oh yeah, and don't forget to sign up on our mailing list (emails rarely happen anyway) and we will give you insider information on new launches, book signings, speaking engagements, and some cool book discounts!

With these notes I bid you adieu, have fun, and good luck!

The 10-Minute or so
Much Ado About Nothing

By William Shakespeare

Creatively modified by Brendan P. Kelso

8-11+ Actors

CAST OF CHARACTERS:

LEONATO – "The Governor"

HERO – Leonato's daughter

BEATRICE – Leonato's niece (funny girl)

DON PEDRO – Prince of Arragon

*BENEDICK – A witty dude who dislikes (likes!) the funny girl

CLAUDIO – Friend to Benedick, in love with Hero

DON JOHN – Brother to Don Pedro – bad guy

**BORACHIO – Evil friend of Don John

*DOGBERRY – A policeman

**FRIAR FRANCIS – A friar named Francis

TOWNSFOLK – Folks from the town

*The same actor who plays Benedick can play Dogberry

**The same actor who plays Borachio can play Friar Francis

MUCH ADO ABOUT NOTHING - The setting: It's the 1600's in a small harbor town on the coast of Italy called Messina. (Think pirates, we like to!)

ACT 1 SCENE 1

(Enter LEONATO, HERO, and BEATRICE)

LEONATO: *(to audience)* I am The Governor. Governor of Messina, Italy.

HERO: Whatever, Dad. You are always talking about yourself. We know you're "The Governor". We've got it. *(sarcastically)* Governor Leonato.

LEONATO: Now listen to me, Hero. You need to behave yourself. We have guests coming. *(BEATRICE laughs at Hero)* And you Beatrice, you better watch your tongue, because I don't want you getting into a "war of words" with Benedick, again. Got me? Look, here comes a message.

(roll of paper, or some type of note flies onto stage)

LEONATO: It says that Don Pedro, the Prince of Arragon, his brother Don John, and his faithful men, Claudio and Benedick, will all be coming soon.

HERO: Oh, goodie! I think Claudio is cute!

BEATRICE: Yeah, well, Benedick is NOT! He's always smelly after a battle!

(enter Don John, Don Pedro, Benedick, and Claudio)

LEONATO: Welcome, Don Pedro and friends! You have fought bravely. Please stay and party with us.

DON PEDRO: We will, thank you!

DON JOHN: *(aside and pouting to the audience)* My brother gets all the attention! I hate him!

DON PEDRO: Don John, what are you saying over there?

DON JOHN: Oh nothing, dear brother. *(starts dancing VERY badly)* Just practicing my dance moves for the party!

BEATRICE: *(mockingly to BENEDICK)* So Benedick, you're back again? *(sniffs him)* And, whew! *(plugging her nose with her fingers)* Smelly as usual.

BENEDICK: *(mockingly in a high girls voice)* "Smelly as usual" You, my dear Beatrice, are a pain as usual. Are you ready to continue our merry war?

BEATRICE: You mean our war of words? You know it!

BENEDICK: You are such a parrot-teacher.

BEATRICE: What did you call me?

BENEDICK: Someone who talks A LOT! What's the matter? Forget your dictionary? You know, *(said slowly as if she doesn't understand English)* PARROT TEACHER.

BEATRICE: Humph! A bird of my tongue is better than a beast of yours!

BENEDICK: I wish my horse had the speed of your tongue!

BEATRICE: *(to audience)* Oh, he makes me sooooo mad! *(BEATRICE stomps her feet like a 4-year old and storms off stage)*

LEONATO: *(to audience)* There's a skirmish of wit between them. *(to all)* Everyone, let's go to my castle. You know, the castle that belongs to The Governor? *(with two thumbs pointing at himself)*

(all exit except CLAUDIO and BENEDICK)

CLAUDIO: *(to BENEDICK)* Hero is sooooooo cute!

BENEDICK: Dude, did you just say, "cute"? No, no, no, NO! A kitten is cute, a baby is cute, but her? No. With a name like "Hero", she can NOT be cute!

CLAUDIO: Yeah, what about her name?

BENEDICK: Come on. "Hero?" Does she drive the Batmobile and wear a cape, too?

CLAUDIO: Leave her alone because...because...because I think I want to marry her!

BENEDICK: Marry? Whoa, buddy! Listen, I mean, she's a bit..... plain. Actually, I do not like her. And as for marriage, it's overrated, so last year. You'll never catch me getting married. That's right, the single life for me!

CLAUDIO: *(CLAUDIO is day dreamy and lovesick)* She is the sweetest lady that I ever looked on. Could you buy such a jewel?

BENEDICK: *(to audience)* And a case to put her into.

(enter DON PEDRO)

DON PEDRO: Where have you guys been?

BENEDICK: You won't believe this! Lovesick Claudio here wants to marry Hero. What a LOSER!

DON PEDRO: Be careful Benedick, my friend. Remember, this is a comedy, and all of Shakespeare's comedies end in marriage.

CLAUDIO: Yeah!

BENEDICK: If I get married, you guys can make fun of me FOREVER! As a matter of fact, this play would change from a comedy to a tragedy, because I think I would die! You two are ridiculous! I'm outta here! *(exits angrily)*

DON PEDRO: Claudio, I'll tell ya what. Tonight there's a masquerade ball. I will attend disguised as you and woo Hero on your behalf. I will get her to fall in love AND agree to get married!

CLAUDIO: Sweet! *(they high five and exit)*

ACT 1 SCENE 3

(enter DON JOHN and BORACHIO)

DON JOHN: Borachio, my friend, I am soooo jealous. I do not like my brother Don Pedro.

BORACHIO: Why?

DON JOHN: *(very upset)* Because everybody likes him, and not me! I would much rather be a canker in a hedge, than a rose in his grace.

BORACHIO: Why?

DON JOHN: Because I am a plain-dealing Villain!

BORACHIO: Why?

DON JOHN: Would you stop asking me that?

BORACHIO: Why?

(DON JOHN pulls his sword on BORACHIO)

BORACHIO: Um...Don John?

DON JOHN: What do you want, Borachio!?!?

BORACHIO: Well sir, it appears that Claudio likes Hero and, your brother, Don Pedro, is going to try and woo her on his behalf.

DON JOHN: *(very calm with an evil look in his eye)* Really?

BORACHIO: Yes, really. Tonight, at the masquerade ball.

DON JOHN: Sweet! *(to the audience)* I will use this to build mischief! You are sure, and will assist me?

BORACHIO: To the death, my lord.

ACT 2 SCENE 1

(enter HERO, LEONATO, BEATRICE)

HERO: I'm excited for the dance!

LEONATO: Remember, daughter, if some guy asks you to marry him, you should say, "Yes".

BEATRICE: Why? What if he's ugly, like Benedick? Men are dirty, smelly, and have prickly beards! I could not endure a husband with a beard on his face.

LEONATO: My niece, thou wilt never get thee a husband, if thou be so shrewd of thy tongue.

BEATRICE: Don't go all "Shakespeare" on me! I am very happy being single, because there is no man good enough for me! I will live as merry as the day is long.

HERO: Oh, here come the guests. The party is starting!

(enter DON PEDRO, CLAUDIO, BENEDICK, DON JOHN, and BORACHIO. Other townsfolk may be here for more dancers; ALL men enter wearing masks)

(It must be clear to the audience, who is whom for the confusion to work!)

DON PEDRO: *(to Hero)* Hey, I think you're cute. Do you want to dance?

HERO: Sure, you seem nice. What's your name?

DON PEDRO: Claudio. *(DON PEDRO lifts mask and winks at the audience; they dance)*

BEATRICE: *(to BENEDICK as they dance badly)* And who are you?

BENEDICK: Uhhhhh....not Benedick.

BEATRICE: You sure dance like him, because he dances like a very dull fool!

BENEDICK: Ouch! That was mean. It's a good thing I'm not Benedick. He would probably say something back like, "You LOOK like a very dull fool!"

(all exit dancing, except DON JOHN, BORACHIO and CLAUDIO, still wearing masks)

DON JOHN: *(to BORACHIO)* Borachio, is that Claudio?

BORACHIO: Yes, I know him by his bearing. *(DON JOHN looks confused)* Bearing.... you know....the way he walks!

DON JOHN: Ohhhhhh..... *(to CLAUDIO)* Are you Benedick?

CLAUDIO: I am he.

DON JOHN: Did you hear that my brother, Don Pedro, is in love with Hero? He plans to ask her to marry him TONIGHT!

CLAUDIO: *(shocked)* WHAT!?!? *(now calm)* I mean, very interesting.

DON JOHN: Yep, I heard him swear his affection.

BORACHIO: So did I too! And he swore he would marry her tonight! Well, we have to go. Bye!

(DON JOHN and BORACHIO exit laughing evilly)

CLAUDIO: *(alone on stage)* NOOOOOOO, THE AGONY!!!! I told him that I was Benedick, but I heard this ill news with the ears of Claudio! Friendship is constant in all other things, except in the affairs of love. Farewell therefore, Hero.

(enter BENEDICK)

BENEDICK: Good news, dude! Don Pedro has won the heart of Hero on your behalf!

CLAUDIO: Apparently Don Pedro wants Hero all to himself. *(exits sulking)*

BENEDICK: *(to audience)* Whoa, what's with Claudio? And what's with Beatrice? Aghhh! Girls! They are so frustrating! *(pointing where Claudio was)* See what happens when you deal with girls?

(enter DON PEDRO)

BENEDICK: Dude, you took Hero for yourself? Claudio sure is bummed.

DON PEDRO: What?! No! Please trust me.

BENEDICK: Okay. But did you see Beatrice insult me during the dance? *(visibly upset)* She called me "the prince's jester" AND a fool! Oh no, here she comes. Please sir, send me away to fetch a tooth-picker from Asia, or to pick a hair off a Pygmy, or to do more homework, please, ANYTHING but to talk with that HARPY!

DON PEDRO: Nah, you need to stay. This is fun!

BENEDICK: I cannot endure my Lady Tongue! I'm outta here!

(exit BENEDICK; enter CLAUDIO, BEATRICE, LEONATO, and HERO)

DON PEDRO: *(to BEATRICE)* Wow! You really made him mad.

BEATRICE: Oh well. I brought you Claudio.

DON PEDRO: Beatrice, go fetch me Hero. *(BEATRICE exits; DON PEDRO faces Claudio)* You look sad.

CLAUDIO: I am.

DON PEDRO: But, I won Hero for you.

CLAUDIO: Seriously? Your brother, Don John, told me that YOU were going to marry her.

LEONATO: You shouldn't listen to Don John. But, yep, she is yours to marry!

CLAUDIO: Sweet! *(they high five)*

(enter BEATRICE with HERO)

BEATRICE: Well, aren't you going to kiss each other?

(CLAUDIO and HERO look at each other and shake their heads 'NO!' emphatically)

BEATRICE: Come on, at least hug. Look, the audience wants to see some romance! *(BEATRICE tries to get the audience involved; CLAUDIO and HERO approach for a hug, but it turns into an awkward high five)*

BEATRICE: *(to audience)* They are silly, yet I am the only one without a husband! Oh well. Later! *(BEATRICE exits)*

DON PEDRO: Okay, the wedding is in a week. In the meantime, let's have some fun! Why don't we get Benedick and Beatrice to fall in love?

ALL: Okay!

HERO: I will do anything to help my cousin to a good husband! *(ALL exit)*

ACT 2 SCENE 2

(enter DON JOHN and BORACHIO)

DON JOHN: Aghhhhhhh! Foiled! That was no fun. They figured out my plot against them!

BORACHIO: I have another idea. Let's convince Don Pedro and Claudio that Hero is unfaithful. My friend Margaret and I will appear outside their window and refer to each other as Hero and Claudio. It's bound to fool them!

DON JOHN: If you can fool them, I will pay you a thousand ducats!

BORACHIO: I don't want any ducks.

DON JOHN: It's silver coins. MONEY!

BORACHIO: Oh! Sounds great! *(starts doing a money dance)* Make money, money, make money, money....Let's go!

(ALL exit)

ACT 2 SCENE 3

(enter BENEDICK)

BENEDICK: *(to audience)* Claudio is a fool. First he says he will not fall in love, and then he falls in love. Here comes the lovesick fool now. I have to hide!

(enter CLAUDIO, DON PEDRO, and LEONATO. They pretend not to notice BENEDICK hiding and peeking at them)

DON PEDRO: So, did you hear that Beatrice is in love with Benedick?

(BENEDICK shows a look of shock to the audience)

CLAUDIO: I did never think that lady would have loved any man.

LEONATO: No, nor I neither. But she does.

BENEDICK: *(to audience)* Neither did I! Is it true? Could she love me?

DON PEDRO: Yeah, but she doesn't want to tell him because she is afraid he will tease her. Oh, well. Stinks to be Benedick!

(DON PEDRO, LEONATO, and CLAUDIO exit laughing with each other)

BENEDICK: *(to audience)* This can be no trick. Wow, she really likes me. I better be nice if I want her to marry me! *(exit)*

ACT 3 SCENE 1

(enter HERO)

HERO: *(to audience)* I sent a messenger to tell Beatrice that I'm talking behind her back. When Beatrice shows up, I am going to trick her into believing that Benedick loves her.

(enter BEATRICE, but she hides)

HERO: *(to the audience in a whisper)* There she is.

HERO: *(now talking to the audience)* Did you hear that Benedick loves Beatrice?

(BEATRICE shows a look of shock to the audience)

HERO: So sad, too bad. Because she doesn't like him!

(HERO exits snickering)

BEATRICE: *(to audience)* Can this be true? I better start being nicer to him! Hmmm, this could be hard. *(exit)*

ACT 3 SCENE 2

(enter DON PEDRO, CLAUDIO, BENEDICK, and LEONATO; BENEDICK is looking really good - he has cleaned up a bit, with no beard)

DON PEDRO: Whoa! Look at you, Benedick. What's up with the combed hair?

CLAUDIO: And the nice threads?

LEONATO: And you shaved? Is there something you're not telling us?

CLAUDIO: *(teasingly)* Could he be in love?

BENEDICK: *(to LEONATO)* Sir, can I have a private word with you, away from these fools?

(exit BENEDICK and LEONATO; enter DON JOHN)

DON JOHN: Hey guys, I have some bad news.

DON PEDRO: What's that, brother?

DON JOHN: Hero, the lady, is disloyal.

CLAUDIO: Who, Hero? MY Hero?

DON JOHN: She's certainly no hero of mine. Yep, I'm talking about YOUR Hero.

DON PEDRO: I will not think it.

DON JOHN: I will prove it. Come with me.

(ALL exit)

ACT 3 SCENE 3

(enter DOGBERRY)

DOGBERRY: *(to the audience)* I am the Police! Tonight I am going to be on watch!

(DOGBERRY is off to the side; enter BORACHIO not noticing DOGBERRY watching him)

BORACHIO: *(to audience)* Do you want to know something funny? My friend, Margaret, and I fooled Don Pedro and Claudio into thinking HERO was unfaithful!

DOGBERRY: You are under arrest for lying to the prince!

BORACHIO: Who, me?

DOGBERRY: Yes, you.

BORACHIO: *(starts running away)* Aghhhhhh!

(chase scene around stage, through the audience, lots of tripping over each other, ending in a dramatic slap fight on stage with the DOGBERRY finally arresting BORACHIO)

DOGBERRY: Come with me!

(DOGBERRY exits dragging BORACHIO off stage)

ACT 3 SCENE 4

(enter HERO and BEATRICE who is off to the side sulking)

HERO: *(excited, addresses audience)* I am getting married today! Beatrice, what's wrong? You seem sick. Oh, I know! You're sick in love with Benedick!

BEATRICE: Oh, I don't feel good.

HERO: You look like you are lovesick.

BEATRICE: Who, me? Never! Well, okay, maybe. But enough about me, let's get you married!

(ALL exit very excited)

ACT 3 SCENE 5

(enter DOGBERRY, and LEONATO)

DOGBERRY: Sir! Sir! I have arrested a man.

LEONATO: Excellent work! What did he do?

DOGBERRY: That's why I am here. It's baaaaaaaad.

LEONATO: Look, I have to go. Just figure out what to do with the criminal yourself. *(ALL exit)*

ACT 4 SCENE 1

(enter DON PEDRO, DON JOHN, LEONATO, FRIAR, CLAUDIO, HERO, BEATRICE, and TOWNSFOLK)

BEATRICE: Friar Francis, let's get this party started!

FRIAR: *(to HERO)* You want to marry this guy?

HERO: I do. *(EVERYONE sighs, "AHHHHH")*

FRIAR: *(to CLAUDIO)* Do you want to marry this lady?

CLAUDIO: No.

HERO: WHAT!?!? *(EVERYONE, "WHAT!?")*

CLAUDIO: You heard me. No. Nope, nada, no way, not gonna happen.

HERO: Oh, I'm not feeling so good.

CLAUDIO: Leonato, take back your daughter! She was unfaithful to me.

DON PEDRO: Yep, she cheated on him! I heard it.

DON JOHN: I heard it, too! *(aside to audience laughing evilly)* Now THIS is fun!

HERO: Uh oh. This is going to be bad. *(HERO faints very melodramatically)*

DON JOHN: We are out of here!

(exit DON JOHN, DON PEDRO, and CLAUDIO; BEATRICE goes to HERO's side; BENEDICK enters)

BEATRICE: Dead, I think! Help, Uncle!

LEONATO: I wish she were dead, rotten kid. Embarrass me, The Governor, in front of the whole town!

FRIAR: Easy there. No way she cheated on Claudio. I know this stuff. After all, I'm a friar.

HERO: *(HERO awakes pleading to her dad)* I swear I did not cheat! If I did, you can torture me to death!

BENEDICK: I think they have been deceived! Tricked!

LEONATO: If that is true, someone is going to pay, BIG TIME! No one, I mean, NO ONE, embarrasses me, The Governor, in front of the whole town. *(gesturing to the audience)*

FRIAR: Hey, I have a cool idea! Let's pretend Hero is dead.

HERO: What!? *(HERO faints again)*

LEONATO: What will this do?

FRIAR: Well, when Claudio hears this, he will realize that he did love her.

LEONATO: And what if it doesn't work? *(HERO starts waking up)*

FRIAR: Then she leaves and becomes a nun. *(HERO gasps and faints again)* So, who's in?

LEONATO: We are. Let's go. *(LEONATO wakes up HERO)*

HERO: But I don't want to be a nun! I look horrible in black, and that wimple thing, eeew, you are NOT getting that on my head!

(exit FRIAR, LEONATO, and HERO)

BENEDICK: Beatrice, I do love nothing in the world so well as you.

BEATRICE: Wow! I feel the same way about you!

BENEDICK: I love you so much, I will do anything for you!

BEATRICE: Great! Then I need you to kill Claudio.

BENEDICK: Hmmmm, let me think about that.... WHAT? Are you out of your mind? I can't quite do that.

BEATRICE: *(putting on her charm)* Then you don't REALLY love me, do you?

BENEDICK: Fine, fine, fine, since you put it that way. I will challenge him ....to the death! *(ALL exit)*

ACT 5 SCENE 1

(enter LEONATO addresses audience)

LEONATO: I am very angry about what Claudio said about my daughter.

(enter CLAUDIO and DON PEDRO)

LEONATO: *(to CLAUDIO)* YOU!!! Let's fight!

DON PEDRO: Do not quarrel with us, good old man.

LEONATO: You slandered the name of The Governor's daughter and now she is DEAD! FIGHT!

CLAUDIO: No.

LEONATO: *(very angry)* I loved my niece, and she is dead, slandered to death by villains! That makes me sooooo angry!

DON PEDRO: He will not fight.

LEONATO: Fine! I'll be back!

(LEONATO exits, very angrily; BENEDICK enters)

BENEDICK: Nice job, guys. You have killed a sweet lady.

DON PEDRO: We feel bad about Hero dying, but she was not faithful to Claudio.

BENEDICK: By the way, Claudio, you and I are going to fight later. Don Pedro, I resign from your service. Oh, yeah, and your brother, Don John? He skipped town. Later!

(exit BENEDICK; enter BORACHIO being escorted by DOGBERRY)

DON PEDRO: *(to BORACHIO)* Guess what? Your captain, Don John, has left, and now you are under arrest!

BORACHIO: *(caves instantly, crying uncontrollably)* I DID IT! I DID IT!

DON PEDRO: *(aside to audience)* What a wimp. *(to BORACHIO)* Did what?

BORACHIO: I have deceived even your very eyes. We pretended that Hero cheated. Don John made us do it!!!

(enter LEONATO)

LEONATO: Who is this guy crying here? Which is the villain?

BORACHIO: I DID IT! I am the one who killed Hero!!! Oh the misery!!! *(on the ground rolling and crying)*

CLAUDIO: *(to LEONATO)* Sir? Umm, we were tricked and made a mistake. We are sorry.

LEONATO: That's okay. This is what I want you to do. Go to her tomb tonight and mourn her death. And in the morning, marry her cousin.

CLAUDIO: That's it?

LEONATO: Yep.

CLAUDIO: Deal! *(they shake on it; ALL exit)*

ACT 5 SCENE 2

(enter BENEDICK and BEATRICE)

BENEDICK: So I challenged Claudio. See, I do love you.

BEATRICE: Sweet! I knew I could believe in you! *(ALL exit)*

ACT 5 SCENE 4

(enter BENEDICK, FRIAR, and LEONATO)

BENEDICK: Hey, Leonato. I think your niece, Beatrice, is cute! So, can I marry her?

LEONATO: My heart is with your liking.

BENEDICK: *(confused)* What?

LEONATO: Yes.

BENEDICK: Sweet!

(enter CLAUDIO and DON PEDRO)

CLAUDIO: Leonato, we have mourned Hero. Now, I will marry her cousin.

LEONATO: You are honorable. *(calls offstage for HERO)* Oh niece, come in here... *(to Claudio)* I think you will like her!

(HERO enters)

CLAUDIO: It's Hero!!!! *(they hug, high five, or some crazy handshake thing kids do)*

BENEDICK: Ha, ha! We tricked you!

CLAUDIO: That's okay. We tricked you guys as well! Now you're getting married to each other. Welcome to a Shakespeare comedy! And the best part is that I get to make fun of you FOREVER!

BEATRICE: WHAT!?!?

BENEDICK: That's okay! I still think she's cute! I really do want to marry her!

BEATRICE: Seriously? You're so sweet. Let's get hitched!

FRIAR: All right all ready. Do you guys and gals want to get married?

BENEDICK, BEATRICE, CLAUDIO, and HERO: Yeah!

FRIAR: Very well. Poof! You're married! You may now kiss, achmmmmm, I mean, high five the brides!

THE END

The 10-Minute or so
Much Ado About Nothing
By William Shakespeare
Creatively modified by Brendan P. Kelso
12-16+ Actors

CAST OF CHARACTERS:

LEONATO – "The Governor"

HERO – Leonato's daughter

BEATRICE – Leonato's niece (funny girl)

ANTONIO – Older brother of Leonato

*MESSENGER – A messenger that delivers a message

DON PEDRO – Prince of Arragon

**BENEDICK – A witty dude who dislikes (likes!) the funny girl

CLAUDIO – Friend to Benedick, in love with Hero

DON JOHN – Brother to Don Pedro – bad guy

BORACHIO – Evil friend of Don John

***CONRADE – Another evil friend of Don John

**DOGBERRY – A policeman

VERGES – A deputy

*WATCHMAN – A watchman

*FRIAR FRANCIS – A friar named Francis

***GRAVEDIGGER – Dude that digs graves

TOWNSFOLK – Folks from the town

*The same actor who plays a Watchman can play the messenger & Friar

**The same actor who plays Benedick can play Dogberry

***The same actor who plays Conrade can play the Gravedigger

MUCH ADO ABOUT NOTHING - The setting: It's the 1600's in a small harbor town on the coast of Italy called Messina. (Think pirates, we like to!)

ACT 1 SCENE 1

(Enter LEONATO, HERO, and BEATRICE)

LEONATO: *(to audience)* I am The Governor. Governor of Messina, Italy.

HERO: Whatever, Dad. You are always talking about yourself. We know you're "The Governor". We've got it. *(sarcastically)* Governor Leonato.

LEONATO: Now listen to me, Hero. You need to behave yourself. We have guests coming. *(BEATRICE laughs at Hero)* And you Beatrice, you better watch your tongue, because I don't want you getting into a "war of words" with Benedick, again. Got me? Look, here comes a messenger.

(enter MESSENGER)

MESSENGER: Sir, I come to tell you that Don Pedro, the Prince of Arragon, his brother Don John, and his faithful men, Claudio and Benedick, will all be coming soon.

(exit MESSENGER)

HERO: Oh, goodie! I think Claudio is cute!

BEATRICE: Yeah, well, Benedick is NOT! He's always smelly after a battle! Oh look, here comes the smelly one now.

(enter Don John, Don Pedro, Benedick, and Claudio)

LEONATO: Welcome, Don Pedro and friends! You have fought bravely. Please stay and party with us.

DON PEDRO: We will, thank you!

DON JOHN: *(aside and pouting to the audience)* My brother gets all the attention! I hate him!

DON PEDRO: Don John, what are you saying over there?

DON JOHN: Oh nothing, dear brother. *(starts dancing VERY badly)* Just practicing my dance moves for the party!

BEATRICE: *(mockingly to BENEDICK)* So Benedick, you're back again? *(sniffs him)* And, whew! *(plugging her nose with her fingers)* Smelly as usual.

BENEDICK: *(mockingly in a high girls voice)* "Smelly as usual" You, my dear Beatrice, are a pain as usual. Are you ready to continue our merry war?

BEATRICE: You mean our war of words? You know it!

BENEDICK: You are such a parrot-teacher.

BEATRICE: What did you call me?

BENEDICK: Someone who talks A LOT! What's the matter? Forget your dictionary? You know, *(said slowly as if she doesn't understand English)* PARROT TEACHER.

BEATRICE: Humph! A bird of my tongue is better than a beast of yours!

BENEDICK: I wish my horse had the speed of your tongue!

BEATRICE: *(to audience)* Oh, he makes me sooooo mad! *(BEATRICE stomps her feet like a 4-year old and storms off stage)*

LEONATO: *(to audience)* There's a skirmish of wit between them. *(to all)* Everyone, let's go to my castle. You know, the castle that belongs to The Governor? *(with two thumbs pointing at himself)*

(all exit except CLAUDIO and BENEDICK)

CLAUDIO: *(to BENEDICK)* Hero is soooooooo cute!

BENEDICK: Dude, did you just say, "cute"? No, no, no, NO! A kitten is cute, a baby is cute, but her? No. With a name like "Hero", she can NOT be cute!

CLAUDIO: Yeah, what about her name?

BENEDICK: Come on. "Hero?" Does she drive the Batmobile and wear a cape, too?

CLAUDIO: Leave her alone because...because...because I think I want to marry her!

BENEDICK: Marry? Whoa, buddy! Listen, I mean, she's a bit..... plain. Actually, I do not like her. And as for marriage, it's overrated, so last year. You'll never catch me getting married. That's right, the single life for me!

CLAUDIO: *(CLAUDIO is day dreamy and lovesick)* She is the sweetest lady that I ever looked on. Could you buy such a jewel?

BENEDICK: *(to audience)* And a case to put her into.

(enter DON PEDRO)

DON PEDRO: Where have you guys been?

BENEDICK: You won't believe this! Lovesick Claudio here wants to marry Hero. What a LOSER!

DON PEDRO: Be careful Benedick, my friend. Remember, this is a comedy, and all of Shakespeare's comedies end in marriage.

CLAUDIO: Yeah!

BENEDICK: If I get married, you guys can make fun of me FOREVER! As a matter of fact, this play would change from a comedy to a tragedy, because I think I would die! You two are ridiculous! I'm outta here! *(exits angrily)*

DON PEDRO: Claudio, I'll tell ya what. Tonight there's a masquerade ball. I will attend disguised as you and woo Hero on your behalf. *(ANTONIO steps on stage and listens in)* I will get her to fall in love AND agree to get married!

CLAUDIO: Sweet! *(they high five and exit)*

ACT 1 SCENE 2

(enter ANTONIO and LEONATO)

ANTONIO: Leonato?

LEONATO: Yes, Antonio, my dear older brother. What have you heard?

ANTONIO: I overheard Don Pedro tell Claudio that he will ask Hero to marry him tonight!

LEONATO: That's confusing. I thought Claudio would want to marry Hero? Oh well.

ANTONIO: Well, that's Shakespeare for you, his comedies are always confusing! You know, this reminds me of another of his plays. I think it was called A Midsummer's Ice Cream, or something like that. Talk about confusion! *(they start talking about the other play as they all exit)* There was this fairy named Puck.... and a donkey!

ACT 1 SCENE 3

(enter DON JOHN and CONRADE)

DON JOHN: Conrade, my friend, I am soooo jealous. I do not like my brother Don Pedro.

CONRADE: Why?

DON JOHN: *(very upset)* Because everybody likes him, and not me! I would much rather be a canker in a hedge, than a rose in his grace.

CONRADE: Why?

DON JOHN: Because I am a plain-dealing Villain!

CONRADE: Why?

DON JOHN: Would you stop asking me that?

CONRADE: Why?

(DON JOHN pulls his sword on CONRADE; BORACHIO enters)

BORACHIO: Sir?

DON JOHN: What do YOU want, Borachio!?!?

BORACHIO: Well sir, it appears that Claudio likes Hero and, your brother, Don Pedro, is going to try and woo her on his behalf.

DON JOHN: *(very calm with an evil look in his eye)* Really?

BORACHIO: Really.

CONRADE: Why?

DON JOHN & BORACHIO: *(to CONRADE)* Stop that!

CONRADE: Sorry.

BORACHIO: *(To DON JOHN)* Yes, tonight, at the masquerade ball.

DON JOHN: Sweet! *(to the audience)* I will use this to build mischief! You are both sure, and will assist me?

BORACHIO: To the death, my lord.

CONRADE: Why? *(DON JOHN and BORACHIO pull their swords and chase CONRADE off stage screaming)*

ACT 2 SCENE 1

(enter HERO, LEONATO, BEATRICE)

HERO: I'm excited for the dance!

LEONATO: Remember, daughter, if some guy asks you to marry him, you should say, "Yes".

BEATRICE: Why? What if he's ugly, like Benedick? Men are dirty, smelly, and have prickly beards! I could not endure a husband with a beard on his face.

LEONATO: My niece, thou wilt never get thee a husband, if thou be so shrewd of thy tongue.

BEATRICE: Don't go all "Shakespeare" on me! I am very happy being single, because there is no man good enough for me! I will live as merry as the day is long.

HERO: Oh, here come the guests. The party is starting!

(enter DON PEDRO, CLAUDIO, BENEDICK, BALTHASAR, DON JOHN, and BORACHIO. Other townsfolk may be here for more dancers; ALL men enter wearing masks)

(It must be clear to the audience, who is whom for the confusion to work!)

DON PEDRO: *(to Hero)* Hey, I think you're cute. Do you want to dance?

HERO: Sure, you seem nice. What's your name?

DON PEDRO: Claudio. *(DON PEDRO lifts mask and winks at the audience; they dance)*

BEATRICE: *(to BENEDICK as they dance badly)* And who are you?

BENEDICK: Uhhhh.....not Benedick.

BEATRICE: You sure dance like him, because he dances like a very dull fool!

BENEDICK: Ouch! That was mean. It's a good thing I'm not Benedick. He would probably say something back like, "You LOOK like a very dull fool!"

(all exit dancing, except DON JOHN, BORACHIO and CLAUDIO, still wearing masks)

DON JOHN: *(to BORACHIO)* Borachio, is that Claudio?

BORACHIO: Yes, I know him by his bearing. *(DON JOHN looks confused)* Bearing.... you know....the way he walks!

DON JOHN: Ohhhhhh..... *(to CLAUDIO)* Are you Benedick?

CLAUDIO: I am he.

DON JOHN: Did you hear that my brother, Don Pedro, is in love with Hero? He plans to ask her to marry him TONIGHT!

CLAUDIO: *(shocked)* WHAT!?!? *(now calm)* I mean, very interesting.

DON JOHN: Yep, I heard him swear his affection.

BORACHIO: So did I too! And he swore he would marry her tonight! Well, we have to go. Bye!

(DON JOHN and BORACHIO exit laughing evilly)

CLAUDIO: *(alone on stage)* NOOOOOOO, THE AGONY!!!! I told him that I was Benedick, but I heard this ill news with the ears of Claudio! Friendship is constant in all other things, except in the affairs of love. Farewell therefore, Hero.

(enter BENEDICK)

BENEDICK: Good news, dude! Don Pedro has won the heart of Hero on your behalf!

CLAUDIO: Apparently Don Pedro wants Hero all to himself. *(exits sulking)*

BENEDICK: *(to audience)* Whoa, what's with Claudio? And what's with Beatrice? Aghhh! Girls! They are so frustrating! *(pointing where Claudio was)* See what happens when you deal with girls?

(enter DON PEDRO)

BENEDICK: Dude, you took Hero for yourself? Claudio sure is bummed.

DON PEDRO: What?! No! Please trust me.

BENEDICK: Okay. But did you see Beatrice insult me during the dance? *(visibly upset)* She called me "the prince's jester" AND a fool! Oh no, here she comes. Please sir, send me away to fetch a tooth-picker from Asia, or to pick a hair off a Pygmy, or to do more homework, please, ANYTHING but to talk with that HARPY!

DON PEDRO: Nah, you need to stay. This is fun!

BENEDICK: I cannot endure my Lady Tongue! I'm outta here!

(exit BENEDICK; enter CLAUDIO, BEATRICE, LEONATO, and HERO)

DON PEDRO: *(to BEATRICE)* Wow! You really made him mad.

BEATRICE: Oh well. I brought you Claudio.

DON PEDRO: Beatrice, go fetch me Hero. *(BEATRICE exits; DON PEDRO faces Claudio)* You look sad.

CLAUDIO: I am.

DON PEDRO: But, I won Hero for you.

CLAUDIO: Seriously? Your brother, Don John, told me that YOU were going to marry her.

LEONATO: You shouldn't listen to Don John. But, yep, she is yours to marry!

CLAUDIO: Sweet! *(they high five)*

(enter BEATRICE with HERO)

BEATRICE: Well, aren't you going to kiss each other?

(CLAUDIO and HERO look at each other and shake their heads 'NO!' emphatically)

BEATRICE: Come on, at least hug. Look, the audience wants to see some romance! *(BEATRICE tries to get the audience involved; CLAUDIO and HERO approach for a hug, but it turns into an awkward high five)*

BEATRICE: *(to audience)* They are silly, yet I am the only one without a husband! Oh well. Later! *(BEATRICE exits)*

DON PEDRO: Okay, the wedding is in a week. In the meantime, let's have some fun! Why don't we get Benedick and Beatrice to fall in love?

ALL: Okay!

HERO: I will do anything to help my cousin to a good husband! *(ALL exit)*

ACT 2 SCENE 2

(enter DON JOHN and BORACHIO)

DON JOHN: Aghhhhhhh! Foiled! That was no fun. They figured out my plot against them!

BORACHIO: I have another idea. Let's convince Don Pedro and Claudio that Hero is unfaithful. My friend Margaret and I will appear outside their window and refer to each other as Hero and Claudio. It's bound to fool them!

DON JOHN: If you can fool them, I will pay you a thousand ducats!

BORACHIO: I don't want any ducks.

DON JOHN: It's silver coins. MONEY!

BORACHIO: Oh! Sounds great! *(starts doing a money dance)* Make money, money, make money, money....Let's go!

(ALL exit)

ACT 2 SCENE 3

(enter BENEDICK)

BENEDICK: *(to audience)* Claudio is a fool. First he says he will not fall in love, and then he falls in love. Here comes the lovesick fool now. I have to hide!

(enter CLAUDIO, DON PEDRO, and LEONATO. They pretend not to notice BENEDICK hiding and peeking at them)

DON PEDRO: So, did you hear that Beatrice is in love with Benedick?

(BENEDICK shows a look of shock to the audience)

CLAUDIO: I did never think that lady would have loved any man.

LEONATO: No, nor I neither. But she does.

BENEDICK: *(to audience)* Neither did I! Is it true? Could she love me?

DON PEDRO: Yeah, but she doesn't want to tell him because she is afraid he will tease her. Oh, well. Stinks to be Benedick!

(DON PEDRO, LEONATO, and CLAUDIO exit laughing with each other)

BENEDICK: *(to audience)* This can be no trick. Wow, she really likes me. I better be nice if I want her to marry me! *(exit)*

ACT 3 SCENE 1

(enter HERO)

HERO: *(to audience)* I sent a messenger to tell Beatrice that I'm talking behind her back. When Beatrice shows up, I am going to trick her into believing that Benedick loves her.

(enter BEATRICE, but she hides)

HERO: *(to the audience in a whisper)* There she is.

HERO: *(now talking to the audience)* Did you hear that Benedick loves Beatrice?

(BEATRICE shows a look of shock to the audience)

HERO: So sad, too bad. Because she doesn't like him!

(HERO exits snickering)

BEATRICE: *(to audience)* Can this be true? I better start being nicer to him! Hmmm, this could be hard. *(exit)*

ACT 3 SCENE 2

(enter DON PEDRO, CLAUDIO, BENEDICK, and LEONATO; BENEDICK is looking really good - he has cleaned up a bit with no beard)

DON PEDRO: Whoa! Look at you, Benedick. What's up with the combed hair?

CLAUDIO: And the nice threads?

LEONATO: And you shaved? Is there something you're not telling us?

CLAUDIO: *(teasingly)* Could he be in love?

BENEDICK: *(to LEONATO)* Sir, can I have a private word with you, away from these fools?

(exit BENEDICK and LEONATO; enter DON JOHN)

DON JOHN: Hey guys, I have some bad news.

DON PEDRO: What's that, brother?

DON JOHN: Hero, the lady, is disloyal.

CLAUDIO: Who, Hero? MY Hero?

DON JOHN: She's certainly no hero of mine. Yep, I'm talking about YOUR Hero.

DON PEDRO: I will not think it.

DON JOHN: I will prove it. Come with me. *(ALL exit)*

ACT 3 SCENE 3

(enter DOGBERRY, VERGES, and WATCHMAN)

DOGBERRY: *(to the audience)* We are the Police! *(to his men)* Are you good men and true? Deputy Verges?

VERGES: Yes sir, Policeman Dogberry!

DOGBERRY: Watchman?

WATCHMAN: Yes, I am!

DOGBERRY: Good, because your job tonight is to watch.

WATCHMAN: Right! *(there's a pause)* Watch what?

DOGBERRY: Just watch.

WATCHMAN: But, if I know what I am watching for, then it would be easier to watch, right?

DOGBERRY: Deputy, will you tell him?

VERGES: Yes sir. You need to watch for.....oh, I don't know... things.

WATCHMAN: What "things", sir? It isn't ghosts, is it? I hope not, because at my last job...

VERGES: *(getting mad)* NOOOOO! Just stand right there and keep your eyes open and stay out of trouble!

WATCHMAN: *(suddenly standing at attention)* Okay!

DOGBERRY: *(to VERGES)* Let's go!

(exit DOGBERRY and VERGES)

WATCHMAN: *(to audience)* You know, at my last job, I really did see a ghost. I worked at this castle in Denmark, great gig, until the king was MURDERED! That's right, DEAD! But what freaked me out was when he came back as a GHOST. Yep, working for Hamlet was really creepy. Wait, here comes someone... *(WATCHMAN hides off to the side; enter BORACHIO and CONRADE not noticing the WATCHMAN watching them)*

BORACHIO: Conrade, do you want to know something funny?

CONRADE: Yeah!

BORACHIO: *(the WATCHMAN is leaning in listening)* Margaret and I fooled Don Pedro and Claudio into thinking HERO was unfaithful!

CONRADE: What? So, let me get this straight. Margaret, acting like she was Hero, convinced Don Pedro and Claudio that she was being unfaithful, and they thought Margaret was Hero?

BORACHIO: The two of them did. We did such a great acting job we even fooled the prince!

WATCHMAN: You two are under arrest for lying to the prince!

CONRADE: Who, us?

WATCHMAN: Yes, you.

BORACHIO: *(to CONRADE)* Let's run for it! Aghhhhh!

(chase scene around stage, through the audience, lots of tripping over each other, ending in a dramatic slap fight on stage with the WATCHMAN finally arresting BORACHIO and CLAUDIO)

WATCHMAN: Come with me!

(ALL exit)

ACT 3 SCENE 4

(enter HERO and BEATRICE who is off to the side sulking)

HERO: *(excited, addresses audience)* I am getting married today! Beatrice, what's wrong? You seem sick. Oh, I know! You're sick in love with Benedick!

BEATRICE: Oh, I don't feel good.

HERO: You look like you are lovesick.

BEATRICE: Who, me? Never! Well, okay, maybe. But enough about me, let's get you married!

(ALL exit very excited)

ACT 3 SCENE 5

(enter DOGBERRY, VERGES, and LEONATO)

DOGBERRY: Sir! Sir! We have arrested two men.

LEONATO: Excellent work! What did they do?

VERGES: That's why we are here. It's baaaaaaaad.

LEONATO: Look, I have to go. Just figure out what to do with the two criminals yourselves. *(ALL exit)*

ACT 4 SCENE 1

(enter DON PEDRO, DON JOHN, LEONATO, FRIAR, CLAUDIO, HERO, BEATRICE, and TOWNSFOLK)

LEONATO: Friar Francis, let's get this party started!

FRIAR: *(to HERO)* You want to marry this guy?

HERO: I do. *(EVERYONE sighs, "AHHHHH")*

FRIAR: *(to CLAUDIO)* Do you want to marry this lady?

CLAUDIO: No.

HERO: WHAT!?!? *(EVERYONE, "WHAT!?")*

CLAUDIO: You heard me. No. Nope, nada, no way, not gonna happen.

HERO: Oh, I'm not feeling so good.

CLAUDIO: Leonato, take back your daughter! She was unfaithful to me.

DON PEDRO: Yep, she cheated on him! I heard it.

DON JOHN: I heard it, too! *(aside to audience laughing evilly)* Now THIS is fun!

HERO: Uh oh. This is going to be bad. *(HERO faints very melodramatically)*

DON JOHN: We are out of here!

(exit DON JOHN, DON PEDRO, and CLAUDIO; BEATRICE goes to HERO's side; enter BENEDICK)

BEATRICE: Dead, I think! Help, Uncle!

LEONATO: I wish she were dead, rotten kid. Embarrass me, The Governor, in front of the whole town!

FRIAR: Easy there. No way she cheated on Claudio. Why, I've known her since she was a baby and she's always been honest and kind...unlike that cousin of hers.

BEATRICE: Hey!

HERO: *(HERO awakes pleading to her dad)* I swear I did not cheat! If I did, you can torture me to death!

BENEDICK: I think they have been deceived! Tricked!

LEONATO: If that is true, someone is going to pay, BIG TIME! No one, I mean, NO ONE, embarrasses me, The Governor, in front of the whole town. *(gesturing to the audience)*

FRIAR: Hey, I have a cool idea! Let's pretend Hero is dead.

HERO: What!? *(HERO faints again)*

LEONATO: What will this do?

FRIAR: Well, when Claudio hears this, he will realize that he did love her.

LEONATO: And what if it doesn't work? *(HERO starts waking up)*

FRIAR: Then she leaves and becomes a nun. *(HERO gasps and faints again)* So, who's in?

LEONATO: We are. Let's go. *(LEONATO wakes up HERO)*

HERO: But I don't want to be a nun! I look horrible in black, and that wimple thing, eeew, you are NOT getting that on my head! *(exit FRIAR, LEONATO, and HERO)*

BENEDICK: Beatrice, I do love nothing in the world so well as you.

BEATRICE: Wow! I feel the same way about you!

BENEDICK: I love you so much! I will do anything for you!

BEATRICE: Great! Then I need you to kill Claudio.

BENEDICK: Hmmmm, let me think about that.... WHAT? Are you out of your mind? I can't quite do that.

BEATRICE: *(putting on her charm)* Then you don't REALLY love me, do you?

BENEDICK: Fine, fine, fine, since you put it that way. I will challenge him ....to the death! *(as he runs off stage with his sword raised!) (ALL exit)*

ACT 5 SCENE 1

(enter LEONATO and ANTONIO)

LEONATO: Brother, I am very angry about what Claudio said about my daughter.

ANTONIO: Me, too!

(enter CLAUDIO and DON PEDRO)

LEONATO: *(to CLAUDIO)* YOU!!! Let's fight!

DON PEDRO: Do not quarrel with us, good old man.

LEONATO: You slandered the name of The Governor's daughter and now she is DEAD! FIGHT!

CLAUDIO: No.

ANTONIO: *(shoves CLAUDIO)* Then you and I will fight, you.... *(trying to find the right word to say)* you... protagonist, you...!

LEONATO: *(a little shocked)* Brother! A protagonist, really?

ANTONIO: *(very angry)* I loved my niece, and she is dead, slandered to death by villains! That makes me sooooo angry!

DON PEDRO: He will not fight.

ANTONIO: Fine! We'll be back!

(LEONATO and ANTONIO exit, very angrily; BENEDICK enters)

BENEDICK: Nice job, guys. You have killed a sweet lady.

DON PEDRO: We feel bad about Hero dying, but she was not faithful to Claudio.

BENEDICK: By the way, Claudio, you and I are going to fight later. Don Pedro, I resign from your service. Oh, yeah, and your brother, Don John? He skipped town. Later!

(exit BENEDICK; enter CONRADE and BORACHIO being escorted by DOGBERRY, VERGES and WATCHMAN)

DON PEDRO: *(to BORACHIO)* Guess what? Your captain, Don John, has left, and now you are under arrest!

BORACHIO & CONRADE: *(caves instantly, crying uncontrollably)* WE DID IT! WE DID IT!

DON PEDRO: *(aside to audience)* What wimps *(to BORACHIO and CONRADE)* Did what?

BORACHIO: We have deceived even your very eyes. We pretended that Hero cheated. Don John made us do it!!!

(enter LEONATO and ANTONIO)

LEONATO: Who are these guys crying here? Which is the villain?

BORACHIO: I AM!

CONRADE: NO! I AM!

BORACHIO: WE BOTH ARE! We are the ones who killed Hero!!! Oh the misery!!! *(BORACHIO and CONRADE are rolling on the ground crying)*

CONRADE: Oh the pain!

CLAUDIO: *(to LEONATO)* Sir? Umm, we were tricked and made a mistake. We are sorry.

LEONATO: That's okay. This is what I want you to do. Go to her tomb tonight and mourn her death. And in the morning, marry her cousin.

CLAUDIO: That's it?

LEONATO: Yep.

CLAUDIO: Deal! *(they shake on it; ALL exit)*

ACT 5 SCENE 2

(enter BENEDICK and BEATRICE)

BENEDICK: So I challenged Claudio. See, I do love you.

BEATRICE: Sweet! I knew I could believe in you! *(ALL exit)*

ACT 5 SCENE 4

(enter BENEDICK, ANTONIO, FRIAR, and LEONATO)

BENEDICK: Hey, Leonato. I think your niece, Beatrice, is cute! So, can I marry her?

LEONATO: My heart is with your liking.

BENEDICK: *(confused)* What?

LEONATO: Yes.

BENEDICK: Sweet!

(enter CLAUDIO and DON PEDRO)

CLAUDIO: Leonato, we have mourned Hero. Now, I will marry her cousin.

LEONATO: You are honorable. Antonio, please get "my niece" for Claudio. *(ANTONIO exits)*

LEONATO: *(to Claudio)* I think you will like her!

(ANTONIO returns with HERO)

CLAUDIO: It's Hero!!!! *(they hug, high five, or some crazy handshake thing kids do)*

BENEDICK: Ha, ha! We tricked you!**CLAUDIO:** That's okay. We tricked you guys as well! Now you're getting married to each other. Welcome to a Shakespeare comedy! And the best part is that I get to make fun of you FOREVER!

BEATRICE: WHAT!?!?

BENEDICK: That's okay! I still think she's cute! I really do want to marry her!

BEATRICE: Seriously? You're so sweet. Let's get hitched!

FRIAR: All right all ready. Do you guys and gals want to get married?

BENEDICK, BEATRICE, CLAUDIO, and HERO: Yeah!

FRIAR: Very well. Poof! You're married! You may now kiss, achmmmmm, I mean, high five the brides!

THE END

The 10-Minute or so
Much Ado About Nothing

By William Shakespeare
Creatively modified by Brendan P. Kelso

16 - 20+ Actors

CAST OF CHARACTERS:

LEONATO – "The Governor"

HERO – Leonato's daughter

BEATRICE – Leonato's niece (funny girl)

ANTONIO – Older brother of Leonato

*****MESSENGER** – A messenger that delivers a message

DON PEDRO – Prince of Arragon

******BENEDICK** – A witty dude who dislikes (likes!) the funny girl

CLAUDIO – Friend to Benedick, in love with Hero

DON JOHN – Brother to Don Pedro – bad guy

BORACHIO – Evil friend of Don John

*******CONRADE** – Another evil friend of Don John

MARGARET – A friend of Hero

URSULA – Another friend of Hero

******DOGBERRY** – A policeman

VERGES – A deputy

*****WATCHMAN 1** – The first watchman

WATCHMAN 2 – The second watchman

*****FRIAR FRANCIS** – A friar named Francis

*******GRAVEDIGGER 1** – Dude that digs graves

GRAVEDIGGER 2 – Another dude that digs graves

TOWNSFOLK – Folks from the town

*The same actor who plays a Watchman can play The Messenger & Friar
**The same actor who plays Benedick can play Dogberry
***The same actor who plays Conrade can play a Gravedigger

MUCH ADO ABOUT NOTHING - The setting: It's the 1600's in a small harbor town on the coast of Italy called Messina. (Think pirates, we like to!)

ACT 1 SCENE 1

(Enter LEONATO, HERO, and BEATRICE)

LEONATO: *(to audience)* I am The Governor. Governor of Messina, Italy.

HERO: Whatever, Dad. You are always talking about yourself. We know you're "The Governor". We've got it. *(sarcastically)* Governor Leonato.

LEONATO: Now listen to me, Hero. You need to behave yourself. We have guests coming. *(BEATRICE laughs at Hero)* And you Beatrice, you better watch your tongue, because I don't want you getting into a "war of words" with Benedick, again. Got me? Look, here comes a messenger.

(enter MESSENGER)

MESSENGER: Sir, I come to tell you that Don Pedro, the Prince of Arragon, his brother Don John, and his faithful men, Claudio and Benedick, will all be coming soon.

(exit MESSENGER)

HERO: Oh, goodie! I think Claudio is cute!

BEATRICE: Yeah, well, Benedick is NOT! He's always smelly after a battle! Oh look, here comes the smelly one now.

(enter Don John, Don Pedro, Benedick, and Claudio)

LEONATO: Welcome, Don Pedro and friends! You have fought bravely. Please stay and party with us.

DON PEDRO: We will, thank you!

DON JOHN: *(aside and pouting to the audience)* My brother gets all the attention! I hate him!

DON PEDRO: Don John, what are you saying over there?

DON JOHN: Oh nothing, dear brother. *(starts dancing VERY badly)* Just practicing my dance moves for the party!

BEATRICE: *(mockingly to BENEDICK)* So Benedick, you're back again? *(sniffs him)* And, whew! *(plugging her nose with her fingers)* Smelly as usual.

BENEDICK: *(mockingly in a high girls voice)* "Smelly as usual" You, my dear Beatrice, are a pain as usual. Are you ready to continue our merry war?

BEATRICE: You mean our war of words? You know it!

BENEDICK: You are such a parrot-teacher.

BEATRICE: What did you call me?

BENEDICK: Someone who talks A LOT! What's the matter? Forget your dictionary? You know, *(said slowly as if she doesn't understand English)* PARROT TEACHER.

BEATRICE: Humph! A bird of my tongue is better than a beast of yours!

BENEDICK: I wish my horse had the speed of your tongue!

BEATRICE: *(to audience)* Oh, he makes me sooooo mad! *(BEATRICE stomps her feet like a 4-year old and storms off stage)*

LEONATO: *(to audience)* There's a skirmish of wit between them. *(to all)* Everyone, let's go to my castle. You know, the castle that belongs to The Governor? *(with two thumbs pointing at himself)*

(all exit except CLAUDIO and BENEDICK)

CLAUDIO: *(to BENEDICK)* Hero is soooooooo cute!

BENEDICK: Dude, did you just say, "cute"? No, no, no, NO! A kitten is cute, a baby is cute, but her? No. With a name like "Hero", she can NOT be cute!

CLAUDIO: Yeah, what about her name?

BENEDICK: Come on, "Hero?" Does she drive the Batmobile and wear a cape, too?

CLAUDIO: Leave her alone because...because...because I think I want to marry her!

BENEDICK: Marry? Whoa, buddy! Listen, I mean, she's a bit..... plain. Actually, I do not like her. And as for marriage, it's overrated, so last year. You'll never catch me getting married. That's right, the single life for me!

CLAUDIO: *(CLAUDIO is day dreamy and lovesick)* She is the sweetest lady that I ever looked on. Could you buy such a jewel?

BENEDICK: *(to audience)* And a case to put her into.

(enter DON PEDRO)

DON PEDRO: Where have you guys been?

BENEDICK: You won't believe this! Lovesick Claudio here wants to marry Hero. What a LOSER!

DON PEDRO: Be careful Benedick, my friend. Remember, this is a comedy, and all of Shakespeare's comedies end in marriage.

CLAUDIO: Yeah!

BENEDICK: If I get married, you guys can make fun of me FOREVER! As a matter of fact, this play would change from a comedy to a tragedy, because I think I would die! You two are ridiculous! I'm outta here!

(BENEDICK exits)

DON PEDRO: Claudio, I'll tell ya what. Tonight there's a masquerade ball. I will attend disguised as you and woo Hero on your behalf. *(ANTONIO steps on stage and listens in)* I will get her to fall in love AND agree to get married!

CLAUDIO: Sweet! *(they high five and exit)*

ACT 1 SCENE 2

(enter ANTONIO and LEONATO)

ANTONIO: Leonato?

LEONATO: Yes, Antonio, my dear older brother. What have you heard?

ANTONIO: I overheard Don Pedro tell Claudio that he will ask Hero to marry him tonight!

LEONATO: That's confusing. I thought Claudio would want to marry Hero? Oh well.

ANTONIO: Well, that's Shakespeare for you, his comedies are always confusing! You know, this reminds me of another of his plays. I think it was called A Midsummer's Ice Cream, or something like that. Talk about confusion! *(they start talking about the other play as they all exit)* There was this fairy named Puck.... and a donkey!

ACT 1 SCENE 3

(enter DON JOHN and CONRADE)

DON JOHN: Conrade, my friend, I am soooo jealous. I do not like my brother Don Pedro.

CONRADE: Why?

DON JOHN: *(very upset)* Because everybody likes him, and not me! I would much rather be a canker in a hedge, than a rose in his grace.

CONRADE: Why?

DON JOHN: Because I am a plain-dealing Villain!

CONRADE: Why?

DON JOHN: Would you stop asking me that?

CONRADE: Why?

(DON JOHN pulls his sword on CONRADE; BORACHIO enters)

BORACHIO: Sir?

DON JOHN: What do YOU want, Borachio!?!?

BORACHIO: Well sir, it appears that Claudio likes Hero and, your brother, Don Pedro, is going to try and woo her on his behalf.

DON JOHN: *(very calm with an evil look in his eye)* Really?

BORACHIO: Really.

CONRADE: Why?

DON JOHN & BORACHIO: *(to CONRADE)* Stop that!

CONRADE: Sorry.

BORACHIO: *(To DON JOHN)* Yes, tonight, at the masquerade ball.

DON JOHN: Sweet! *(to the audience)* I will use this to build mischief! You are both sure, and will assist me?

BORACHIO: To the death, my lord.

CONRADE: Why? *(DON JOHN and BORACHIO pull their swords and chase CONRADE off stage screaming)*

ACT 2 SCENE 1

(enter HERO, LEONATO, BEATRICE)

HERO: I'm excited for the dance!

LEONATO: Remember, daughter, if some guy asks you to marry him, you should say, "Yes".

BEATRICE: Why? What if he's ugly, like Benedick? Men are dirty, smelly, and have prickly beards! I could not endure a husband with a beard on his face.

LEONATO: My niece, thou wilt never get thee a husband, if thou be so shrewd of thy tongue.

BEATRICE: Don't go all "Shakespeare" on me! I am very happy being single, because there is no man good enough for me! I will live as merry as the day is long.

HERO: Oh, here come the guests. The party is starting!

(enter DON PEDRO, CLAUDIO, BENEDICK, BALTHASAR, DON JOHN, MARGARET, URSULA, and BORACHIO. Other townsfolk may be here for more dancers; ALL men enter wearing masks)

(It must be clear to the audience, who is whom for the confusion to work!)

DON PEDRO: *(to Hero)* Hey, I think you're cute. Do you want to dance?

HERO: Sure, you seem nice. What's your name?

DON PEDRO: Claudio. *(DON PEDRO lifts mask and winks at the audience; they dance)*

BEATRICE: *(to BENEDICK as they dance badly)* And who are you?

BENEDICK: Uhhhhh......not Benedick.

BEATRICE: You sure dance like him, because he dances like a very dull fool!

BENEDICK: Ouch! That was mean. It's a good thing I'm not Benedick. He would probably say something back like, "You LOOK like a very dull fool!"

(all exit dancing, except DON JOHN, BORACHIO and CLAUDIO, still wearing masks)

DON JOHN: *(to BORACHIO)* Borachio, is that Claudio?

BORACHIO: Yes, I know him by his bearing.*(DON JOHN looks confused)* Bearing.... you know....the way he walks!

DON JOHN: Ohhhhhh..... *(to CLAUDIO)* Are you Benedick?

CLAUDIO: I am he.

DON JOHN: Did you hear that my brother, Don Pedro, is in love with Hero? He plans to ask her to marry him TONIGHT!

CLAUDIO: *(shocked)* WHAT!?!? *(now calm)* I mean, very interesting.

DON JOHN: Yep, I heard him swear his affection.

BORACHIO: So did I too! And he swore he would marry her tonight! Well, we have to go. Bye!

(DON JOHN and BORACHIO exit laughing evilly)

CLAUDIO: *(alone on stage)* NOOOOOOO, THE AGONY!!!! I told him that I was Benedick, but I heard this ill news with the ears of Claudio! Friendship is constant in all other things, except in the affairs of love. Farewell therefore, Hero.

(enter BENEDICK)

BENEDICK: Good news, dude! Don Pedro has won the heart of Hero on your behalf!

CLAUDIO: Apparently Don Pedro wants Hero all to himself. *(exits sulking)*

BENEDICK: *(to audience)* Whoa, what's with Claudio? And what's with Beatrice? Aghhh! Girls! They are so frustrating! *(pointing where Claudio was)* See what happens when you deal with girls?

(enter DON PEDRO)

BENEDICK: Dude, you took Hero for yourself? Claudio sure is bummed.

DON PEDRO: What?! No! Please trust me.

BENEDICK: Okay. But did you see Beatrice insult me during the dance? *(visibly upset)* She called me "the prince's jester", AND a fool! Oh no, here she comes. Please sir, send me away to fetch a tooth-picker from Asia, or to pick a hair off a Pygmy, or to do more homework, please, ANYTHING but to talk with that HARPY!

DON PEDRO: Nah, you need to stay. This is fun!

BENEDICK: I cannot endure my Lady Tongue! I'm outta here! *(exits angrily)*

(enter CLAUDIO, BEATRICE, LEONATO, and HERO)

DON PEDRO: *(to BEATRICE)* Wow! You really made him mad.

BEATRICE: Oh well. I brought you Claudio.

DON PEDRO: Beatrice, go fetch me Hero. *(BEATRICE exits; DON PEDRO faces Claudio)* You look sad.

CLAUDIO: I am.

DON PEDRO: But, I won Hero for you.

CLAUDIO: Seriously? Your brother, Don John, told me that YOU were going to marry her.

LEONATO: You shouldn't listen to Don John. But, yep, she is yours to marry!

CLAUDIO: Sweet! *(they high five)*

(enter BEATRICE with HERO)

BEATRICE: Well, aren't you going to kiss each other?

(CLAUDIO and HERO look at each other and shake their heads 'NO!' emphatically)

BEATRICE: Come on, at least hug. Look, the audience wants to see some romance! *(BEATRICE tries to get the audience involved; CLAUDIO and HERO approach for a hug, but it turns into an awkward high five)*

BEATRICE: *(to audience)* They are silly, yet I am the only one without a husband! Oh well. Later! *(BEATRICE exits)*

DON PEDRO: Okay, the wedding is in a week. In the meantime, let's have some fun! Why don't we get Benedick and Beatrice to fall in love?

ALL: Okay!

HERO: I will do anything to help my cousin to a good husband! *(ALL exit)*

ACT 2 SCENE 2

(enter DON JOHN and BORACHIO)

DON JOHN: Aghhhhhhh! Foiled! That was no fun. They figured out my plot against them!

BORACHIO: I have another idea. Let's convince Don Pedro and Claudio that Hero is unfaithful. My friend Margaret and I will appear outside their window and refer to each other as Hero and Claudio. It's bound to fool them!

DON JOHN: If you can fool them, I will pay you a thousand ducats!

BORACHIO: I don't want any ducks.

DON JOHN: It's silver coins. MONEY!

BORACHIO: Oh! Sounds great! *(starts doing a money dance)* Make money, money, make money, money....Let's go!

(ALL exit)

ACT 2 SCENE 3

(enter BENEDICK)

BENEDICK: *(to audience)* Claudio is a fool. First he says he will not fall in love, and then he falls in love. Here comes the lovesick fool now. I have to hide!

(enter CLAUDIO, DON PEDRO, and LEONATO. They pretend not to notice BENEDICK hiding and peeking at them)

DON PEDRO: So, did you hear that Beatrice is in love with Benedick?

(BENEDICK shows a look of shock to the audience)

CLAUDIO: I did never think that lady would have loved any man.

LEONATO: No, nor I neither. But she does.

BENEDICK: *(to audience)* Neither did I! Is it true? Could she love me?

DON PEDRO: Yeah, but she doesn't want to tell him because she is afraid he will tease her. Oh, well. Stinks to be Benedick!

(DON PEDRO, LEONATO, and CLAUDIO exit laughing with each other)

BENEDICK: *(to audience)* This can be no trick. Wow, she really likes me. I better be nice if I want her to marry me! *(exit)*

ACT 3 SCENE 1

(enter HERO, URSULA, and MARGARET)

HERO: Margaret, go tell Beatrice that Ursula and I are talking behind her back.

MARGARET: Okay.

(exit MARGARET)

HERO: Ursula, when Beatrice shows up, we are going to trick her into believing that Benedick loves her. Cool?

URSULA: Cool!

(enter BEATRICE, but she hides)

HERO: *(aside to audience)* There she is.

URSULA: So Hero, did you hear that Benedick loves Beatrice?

HERO: Yes, I heard the prince, Don Pedro, say that, too!

(BEATRICE shows a look of shock to the audience)

URSULA: So sad, too bad.

HERO: Why?

URSULA: Well, he is such a proud man! He is afraid to tell her because she might start insulting him again. It's so sad.

HERO: And he is such a nice and good-looking guy, too. It's just too bad!

URSULA: See! I just told you – so sad, too bad!

(exit HERO and URSULA)

BEATRICE: *(to audience)* Can this be true? I better start being nicer to him! Hmmm, this could be hard. *(exit)*

ACT 3 SCENE 2

(enter DON PEDRO, CLAUDIO, BENEDICK, and LEONATO; BENEDICK is looking really good - he cleaned up a bit, with no beard)

DON PEDRO: Whoa! Look at you, Benedick. What's up with the combed hair?

CLAUDIO: And the nice threads?

LEONATO: And you shaved? Is there something you're not telling us?

CLAUDIO: *(teasingly)* Could he be in love?

BENEDICK: *(to LEONATO)* Sir, can I have a private word with you, away from these fools?

(exit BENEDICK and LEONATO; enter DON JOHN)

DON JOHN: Hey guys, I have some bad news.

DON PEDRO: What's that, brother?

DON JOHN: Hero, the lady, is disloyal.

CLAUDIO: Who, Hero? MY Hero?

DON JOHN: She's certainly no hero of mine. Yep, I'm talking about YOUR Hero.

DON PEDRO: I will not think it.

DON JOHN: I will prove it. Come with me. *(ALL exit)*

ACT 3 SCENE 3

(enter DOGBERRY, VERGES, and WATCHMAN 1 & 2)

DOGBERRY: *(to the audience)* We are the Police! *(to his men)* Are you good men and true? Deputy Verges?

VERGES: Yes sir, Policeman Dogberry!

DOGBERRY: Watchmen?

WATCHMAN 1 & 2: Yes, we are!

DOGBERRY: Good, because your job tonight is to watch.

WATCHMAN 1: Right! *(there's a pause)* Watch what?

DOGBERRY: Just watch.

WATCHMAN 2: But, if we know what we are watching for, then it would be easier to watch, right?

WATCHMAN 1: *(nodding in agreement)* Yeah, what he said!

DOGBERRY: Deputy, will you tell them?

VERGES: Yes sir. You need to watch for.....oh, I don't know... things.

WATCHMAN 1: What "things", sir?

WATCHMAN 2: It isn't ghosts, is it?

WATCHMAN 1: Ghosts? No, no, no. We need to be on the look out for witches!

VERGES: *(getting mad)* NOOOOO! Just stand right there and keep your eyes open and stay out of trouble!

WATCHMAN 1 & 2: *(suddenly standing at attention)* Okay!

DOGBERRY: *(to VERGES)* Let's go!

(exit DOGBERRY and VERGES)

WATCHMAN 2: You know, I've been watching out for ghosts for years now. It all started when I worked for this king in Denmark named Hamlet.

WATCHMAN 1: Yeah? Hamlet? That's a strange name for a king. When I was in Scotland, the towns were called hamlets.

WATCHMAN 2: Towns named hamlets? That's strange. Yeah, his name was Hamlet. His son was named Hamlet, too. Anyway, he was murdered and came back as a ghost.

WATCHMAN 1: No way!

WATCHMAN 2: Way! I'll tell you, working for King Hamlet was a creepy job!

WATCHMAN 1: Sounds creepy. I once worked up in Scotland for this guy who hung out with 3 smelly witches. I think I'd rather deal with a ghost than witches.

WATCHMAN 2: Really?

WATCHMAN 1: Really. Yeah, my boss, Macbeth, went crazy and then he... wait, here comes something. I hope it's not something wicked. Those witches were always saying something wicked was coming!

(WATCHMEN hide off to the side)

BORACHIO: Conrade, do you want to know something funny?

CONRADE: Yeah!

BORACHIO: Margaret and I fooled Don Pedro and Claudio into thinking HERO was unfaithful!

CONRADE: What? So, let me get this straight. Margaret, acting like she was Hero, convinced Don Pedro and Claudio that she was being unfaithful, and they thought Margaret was Hero?

BORACHIO: The two of them did. We did such a great acting job we even fooled the prince!

WATCHMAN 1: You two are under arrest for lying to the prince!

CONRADE: Who, us?

WATCHMAN 2: Yes, you.

BORACHIO: *(to CONRADE)* Let's run for it!

(chase scene around stage, through the audience, lots of tripping over each other, ending in a dramatic slap fight on stage with the WATCHMEN finally arresting BORACHIO and CLAUDIO)

WATCHMAN 1: Come with us! *(ALL exit)*

ACT 3 SCENE 4

(enter HERO, URSULA, MARGARET, and BEATRICE who is off to the side sulking)

HERO: *(excited)* I am getting married today! *(all do a high five or group cheer together, except BEATRICE)*

MARGARET: Beatrice, what's wrong? You seem sick.

HERO: Yes, she's sick all right. Sick in love with Benedick!

BEATRICE: Oh, I don't feel good.

MARGARET: You look like you are lovesick.

BEATRICE: Who, me? Never! Well, okay, maybe.

URSULA: Hey, ladies, we have to go! Remember, someone's getting married today!

(ALL exit very excited)

ACT 3 SCENE 5

(enter DOGBERRY, VERGES, and LEONATO)

DOGBERRY: Sir, sir! We have arrested two men.

LEONATO: Excellent work! What did they do?

VERGES: That's why we are here. It's baaaaaaaad.

LEONATO: Look, I have to go. Just figure out what to do with the two criminals yourselves. *(ALL exit)*

ACT 4 SCENE 1

(enter DON PEDRO, DON JOHN, LEONATO, FRIAR, CLAUDIO, BENEDICK, HERO, BEATRICE, and TOWNSFOLK)

BENEDICK: Friar Francis, let's get this party started!

FRIAR: *(to HERO)* You want to marry this guy?

HERO: I do. *(EVERYONE sighs, "AHHHHH")*

FRIAR: *(to CLAUDIO)* Do you want to marry this lady?

CLAUDIO: No.

HERO: WHAT!?!? *(EVERYONE, "WHAT!?")*

CLAUDIO: You heard me, no. Nope, nada, no way, not gonna happen.

HERO: Oh, I'm not feeling so good.

CLAUDIO: Leonato, take back your daughter! She was unfaithful to me.

DON PEDRO: Yep, she cheated on him! I heard it.

DON JOHN: I heard it, too! *(aside to audience laughing evilly)* Now THIS is fun!

HERO: Uh oh. This is going to be bad. *(HERO faints very melodramatically)*

DON JOHN: We are out of here!

(exit DON JOHN, DON PEDRO, and CLAUDIO; BEATRICE goes to HERO's side)

BEATRICE: Dead, I think! Help, Uncle!

LEONATO: I wish she were dead, rotten kid. Embarrass me, The Governor, in front of the whole town!

FRIAR: Easy there. No way she cheated on Claudio. I know this stuff. After all, I'm a friar.

HERO: *(HERO awakes pleading to her dad)* I swear I did not cheat! If I did, you can torture me to death!

BENEDICK: I think they have been deceived! Tricked!

LEONATO: If that is true, someone is going to pay, BIG TIME! No one, I mean NO ONE, embarasses me, The Governor, in front of the whole town. *(geasturing to the audience)*

FRIAR: Hey, I have a cool idea! Let's pretend Hero is dead.

HERO: What!? *(HERO faints again)*

LEONATO: What will this do?

FRIAR: Well, when Claudio hears this, he will realize that he did love her.

LEONATO: And what if it doesn't work? *(HERO starts waking up)*

FRIAR: Then she leaves and becomes a nun. *(HERO gasps and faints again)* So, who's in?

LEONATO: We are. Let's go. *(LEONATO wakes up HERO then exits holding HERO'S arm)*

HERO: But I don't want to be a nun! I look horrible in black, and that wimple thing, ewe, you are NOT getting that on my head!

(exit FRIAR, LEONATO, and HERO)

BENEDICK: Beatrice, I do love nothing in the world so well as you.

BEATRICE: Wow! I feel the same way about you!

BENEDICK: I love you so much, I will do anything for you!

BEATRICE: Great! Then I need you to kill Claudio.

BENEDICK: Hmmmm, let me think about that.... WHAT? Are you out of your mind? I can't quite do that.

BEATRICE: *(putting on her charm)* Then you don't REALLY love me, do you?

BENEDICK: Fine, fine, fine, since you put it that way. I will challenge him ....to the death! *(ALL exit)*

ACT 5 SCENE 1

(enter LEONATO and ANTONIO)

LEONATO: Brother, I am very angry about what Claudio said about my daughter.

ANTONIO: Me, too!

(enter CLAUDIO and DON PEDRO)

LEONATO: *(to CLAUDIO)* YOU!!! Let's fight!

DON PEDRO: Do not quarrel with us, good old man.

LEONATO: You slandered my daughter's name and now she is DEAD! FIGHT!

CLAUDIO: No.

ANTONIO: *(shoves CLAUDIO)* Then you and I will fight, you.... *(trying to find the right word to say)* you... protagonist, you...!

LEONATO: *(a little shocked)* Brother! A protagonist, really?

ANTONIO: *(very angry)* I loved my niece, and she is dead, slandered to death by villains! That makes me sooooo angry!

DON PEDRO: He will not fight.

ANTONIO: Fine! We'll be back!

(LEONATO and ANTONIO exit, very angrily; BENEDICK enters)

BENEDICK: Nice job, guys. You have killed a sweet lady.

DON PEDRO: We feel bad about Hero dying, but she was not faithful to Claudio.

BENEDICK: By the way, Claudio, you and I are going to fight later. Don Pedro, I resign from your service. Oh, yeah, and your brother, Don John? He skipped town. Later!

(exit BENEDICK; enter CONRADE and BORACHIO being escorted by DOGBERRY, VERGES and WATCHMEN)

DON PEDRO: *(to BORACHIO)* Guess what? Your captain, Don John, has left, and now you are under arrest!

BORACHIO & CONRADE: *(caves instantly, crying uncontrollably)* WE DID IT! WE DID IT!

DON PEDRO: *(aside to audience)* What wimps *(to BORACHIO and CONRADE)* Did what?

BORACHIO: We have deceived even your very eyes. We pretended that Hero cheated. Don John made us do it!!!

(enter LEONATO and ANTONIO)

LEONATO: Who are these guys crying here? Which is the villain?

BORACHIO: I AM!

CONRADE: NO! I AM!

BORACHIO: WE BOTH ARE! We are the ones who killed Hero!!! Oh the misery!!! *(BORACHIO and CONRADE are rolling on the ground crying)*

CONRADE: Oh the pain!

CLAUDIO: *(to LEONATO)* Sir? Umm, we were tricked and made a mistake. We are sorry.

LEONATO: That's okay. This is what I want you to do. Go to her tomb tonight and mourn her death. And in the morning, marry her cousin.

CLAUDIO: That's it?

LEONATO: Yep.

CLAUDIO: Deal! *(they shake on it; ALL exit)*

ACT 5 SCENE 2

(enter BENEDICK and BEATRICE)

BENEDICK: So I challenged Claudio. See, I do love you.

BEATRICE: Sweet! I knew I could believe in you!

(enter URSULA)

URSULA: Guess what?

BENEDICK and BEATRICE: What?!

URSULA: Hero is innocent! Claudio was tricked.

BENEDICK and BEATRICE: Yea! Let's go to the wedding!

(ALL exit)

ACT 5 SCENE 4

(enter BENEDICK, ANTONIO, MARGARET, URSULA, FRIAR, and LEONATO)

BENEDICK: Hey, Leonato. I think your niece, Beatrice, is cute! So, can I marry her?

LEONATO: My heart is with your liking.

BENEDICK: *(confused)* What?

LEONATO: Yes.

BENEDICK: Sweet!

(enter CLAUDIO and DON PEDRO)

CLAUDIO: Okay Leonato, we have mourned Hero. Now, I will marry her cousin.

LEONATO: You are honorable. Antonio, please get "my niece" for Claudio. *(ANTONIO exits)*

LEONATO: *(to Claudio)* I think you will like her!

(ANTONIO returns with HERO)

CLAUDIO: It's Hero!!!! *(they hug, hive five, or some crazy handshake thing kids do)*

BENEDICK: Ha, ha! We tricked you!

CLAUDIO: That's okay. We tricked you guys as well! Now you're getting married to each other. Welcome to a Shakespeare comedy! And the best part, I get to make fun of you FOREVER!

BEATRICE: WHAT!?!?

BENEDICK: That's okay! I still think she's cute! I really do want to marry her!

BEATRICE: Seriously? You're so sweet. Let's get hitched!

FRIAR: All right all ready, do you guys and gals want to get married?

BENEDICK, BEATRICE, CLAUDIO, and HERO: Yeah!

FRIAR: Very well. Poof! You're married! You may now kiss, achmmmmm, I mean, high five the brides!

THE END

Notes

18660445R00039

Made in the USA
San Bernardino, CA
23 January 2015